PLANT-BASED MEDITERRANEAN DIET COOKBOOK

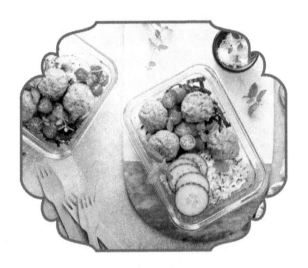

The Comprehensive Guide to Delicious and Nutrient Packed Recipes for Lasting Weight Loss and Healthy Lifestyle

KEVIN S. MAXWELL

EMAIL ME!

I know that exploring topics that involve food and nutrition can often lead to questions and uncertainty. I invite you to contact me with any questions you may have. I'm here to assist.

Please contact me through email at **kevinmaxwelldiet@gmail.com**, and I will try my best to respond to you within 24 hours.

Additionally, if you are interested in exploring other collections of my books.
You can check out additional collections of my books by scanning the QR Code that is provided below.

TABLE OF CONTENT

INTRODUCTION
CHAPTER 1: MEDITERRANEAN DIET
WHAT IS THE MEDITERRANEAN DIET
TIPS TO ACHIEVE OPTIMAL HEALTH WITH
THE MEDITERRANEAN DIET
CHAPTER 2: BENEFITS OF FOLLOWING
MEDITERRANEAN DIET
HOW TO FOLLOW MEDITERRANEAN DIET
CHAPTER 3: LIST OF INGREDIENTS
CHAPTER 4: HEALTHY RECIPES
BREAKFAST
    Recipe 1: Mediterranean Stuffed Avocado
    Recipe 2: Mediterranean Chia Seed Pudding
    Recipe 3: Mediterranean Breakfast
    Bruschetta
    Recipe 4: Mediterranean Breakfast Burrito
    Recipe 5: Greek-Inspired Overnight Oats
LUNCH
    Recipe 1: Mediterranean Quinoa Salad
    Recipe 2: Mediterranean Chickpea and
    Vegetable Skewers
    Recipe 3: Mediterranean Stuffed Bell
    Peppers
    Recipe 4: Greek Chickpea Salad Wraps
    Recipe 5: Mediterranean Lentil Soup
SNACKS
    Recipe 1: Hummus and Veggie Platter
    Recipe 2: Mediterranean Stuffed Grape
    Leaves
    Recipe 3: Greek Salad Skewers

Recipe 4: Roasted Red Pepper and Walnut Dip

Recipe 5: Mediterranean Fruit Salad

DINNER

Recipe 1: Mediterranean Chickpea and Spinach Stew

Recipe 2: Stuffed Portobello Mushrooms

Recipe 3: Mediterranean Lentil and Vegetable Stir-Fry

Recipe 4: Greek-Inspired Couscous Salad

Recipe 5: Eggplant and Tomato Bake

DESSERT

Recipe 1: Mediterranean Fruit Salad with Mint

Recipe 2: Greek Yogurt Parfait with Pistachios and Honey

Recipe 3: Almond and Orange Blossom Cookies

Recipe 4: Date and Walnut Energy Bites

Recipe 5: Vegan Lemon Sorbet

CHAPTER 5: MEAL PLANNING

Benefits of Meal Planning

Tips for Effective Meal Planning

14-DAY MEAL PLAN

CONCLUSION

BONUS: WEEKLY MEAL PLANNER/ JOURNAL

INTRODUCTION

In the heart of Serenity Bay, a coastal town embraced by the gentle whispers of the sea, lived a man named Oliver. Working tirelessly as a software engineer, Oliver found himself caught in the web of unhealthy habits and an expanding waistline. Yearning for a change, he stumbled upon a culinary revelation that would not only transform his physique but also redefine his relationship with food.

One day, while wandering through the shelves of the local bookstore, Oliver discovered a cookbook that promised a path to health through the flavors of the Mediterranean. Titled "Plant-Based Mediterranean Delights," it became his beacon of hope. Filled with vibrant recipes that celebrated fresh ingredients, aromatic herbs, and the simplicity of plant-based goodness, the cookbook captured Oliver's imagination.

Determined to break free from his sedentary lifestyle and unhealthy eating patterns, Oliver embraced the cookbook's offerings. He delved into the world of colorful vegetables, hearty legumes, and nourishing grains. Olive oil, once a mere condiment, now took center stage in his kitchen, replacing the processed ingredients that had long overstayed their welcome.

The journey towards a healthier life unfolded as Oliver immersed himself in the joy of cooking. Each recipe became a culinary adventure, a celebration of flavors inspired by the diverse landscapes of the Mediterranean. From crisp salads infused with the essence of summer to robust stews warming the chill of winter, Oliver discovered a symphony of tastes that resonated with his newfound commitment to well-being.

With every bite, Oliver felt a transformation within. His energy levels soared, his skin glowed with vitality, and a sense of lightness replaced the heaviness that had burdened him for far too long. The plant-based Mediterranean diet not only managed his weight but also elevated his mood and sharpened his focus.

As the seasons changed, so did Oliver's menu. The cookbook guided him through a harmonious rhythm of culinary exploration, aligning with the availability of fresh produce each month. Oliver's kitchen became a sanctuary where the fragrances of Mediterranean herbs and spices danced in the air, and the clinking of pots and pans echoed the joy of nourishing both body and soul.

Word of Oliver's transformation spread throughout Serenity Bay. Friends and family, once skeptical, now marveled at his newfound vitality and zest for life. Inspired by his journey, others in the community embraced the plant-based Mediterranean lifestyle, creating a ripple effect of health and well-being.

In the heart of Serenity Bay, Oliver's story unfolded as a testament to the transformative power of a well-balanced, plant-based Mediterranean diet. It was a journey that not only reshaped his body but also revitalized his spirit, leaving an indelible mark on the town and inspiring others to embark on their path to a healthier, more vibrant life.

CHAPTER 1: MEDITERRANEAN DIET

WHAT IS THE MEDITERRANEAN DIET

The Mediterranean Diet, celebrated for its health benefits and delicious flavors, is a lifestyle that draws inspiration from the traditional eating patterns of countries surrounding the Mediterranean Sea. It emphasizes whole, nutrient-rich foods, and a harmonious balance between various food groups. When exploring the Mediterranean Diet a Plant-Based Mediterranean Cookbook, one discovers a wealth of culinary treasures that not only promote well-being but also elevate the dining experience to a celebration of fresh, wholesome ingredients.

At the core of the Mediterranean Diet is a focus on plant-based foods. The Plant-Based Mediterranean Cookbook takes this principle to heart, offering a diverse array of recipes centered around vegetables, fruits, legumes, nuts, and whole grains. These ingredients form the foundation of meals, providing essential vitamins, minerals, and antioxidants that contribute to overall health. The cookbook becomes a guide, weaving a tapestry of flavors that reflect the abundance of nature and the vibrant colors of the Mediterranean landscape.

Olive oil, a staple in the Mediterranean Diet, takes a prominent role in the cookbook's recipes. Known for its heart-healthy monounsaturated fats, olive oil not only adds richness to dishes but also imparts a distinct, savory flavor. From drizzling over salads to sautéing vegetables, the cookbook demonstrates the versatility of olive oil, elevating the taste profile of each recipe while adhering to the diet's principles.

The use of herbs and spices in the Plant-Based Mediterranean Cookbook further enhances the sensory experience.

Inspired by the Mediterranean tradition, herbs like basil, oregano, rosemary, and thyme infuse dishes with robust flavors, minimizing the need for excessive salt or unhealthy seasonings. This approach aligns seamlessly with the Mediterranean Diet, emphasizing the importance of flavoring food with natural, aromatic ingredients.

The inclusion of plant-based proteins, such as legumes and nuts, is another cornerstone of the Mediterranean Diet. The cookbook provides inventive ways to incorporate these protein sources into meals, ensuring a satisfying and nutritious dining experience. From chickpea-based stews to nutty salads, the recipes showcase the diversity of plant-based proteins, contributing to the diet's reputation for promoting heart health and longevity.

The celebration of seasonal produce is a guiding principle in both the Mediterranean Diet and the Plant-Based Mediterranean Cookbook. By aligning meals with the availability of fresh, local ingredients, the cookbook encourages a connection with nature's cycles. This not only enhances the flavors of each dish but also ensures a varied and nutrient-dense diet throughout the year.

The Plant-Based Mediterranean Cookbook, through its thoughtful curation of recipes, transforms the Mediterranean Diet into a culinary journey. It demonstrates that embracing a plant-based approach doesn't mean sacrificing flavor or satisfaction. Instead, it opens the door to a world of gastronomic delights that nourish the body and tantalize the taste buds.

In essence, the relationship between the Mediterranean Diet and the Plant-Based Mediterranean Cookbook is one of synergy and culinary artistry. Through mindful selection and preparation of ingredients, the cookbook embodies the core principles of the Mediterranean Diet, making it not just a collection of recipes but a guide to a vibrant and wholesome lifestyle that stands as a testament to the richness of Mediterranean culinary traditions.

TIPS TO ACHIEVE OPTIMAL HEALTH WITH THE MEDITERRANEAN DIET

The Mediterranean Diet, renowned for its health benefits, places emphasis on a balanced and plant-centric approach to eating. In the context of optimizing health, the Plant-Based Mediterranean Cookbook becomes a valuable companion, offering a treasure trove of recipes that align with the diet's principles. To achieve optimum health, understanding the foods to eat and avoid is essential, and this cookbook becomes a guide to crafting meals that not only nourish the body but also tantalize the taste buds.

The foundation of a Mediterranean Diet lies in whole, minimally processed foods. The Plant-Based Mediterranean Cookbook echoes this principle by highlighting the abundance of plant-derived ingredients. Colorful vegetables, rich in vitamins, minerals, and antioxidants, take center stage in recipes ranging from vibrant salads to hearty stews. These vegetables not only contribute to optimum health but also add a spectrum of flavors and textures to meals, making plant-based eating a delightful experience.

Fruits, another cornerstone of the Mediterranean Diet, find their place in the cookbook's recipes. From refreshing citrus salads to fruity desserts, the cookbook showcases inventive ways to incorporate nature's sweet offerings. Fruits provide essential nutrients and natural sugars, healthfully satisfying sweet cravings.

Whole grains, such as quinoa, bulgur, and farro, are celebrated in both the Mediterranean Diet and the cookbook. These grains form the basis of nourishing dishes, offering complex carbohydrates, fiber, and various micronutrients. The cookbook's creative use of whole grains demonstrates that healthy eating need not be bland but can be a culinary adventure, satisfying the palate while promoting long-term well-being.

Legumes, including beans, lentils, and chickpeas, are plant-based protein sources integral to the Mediterranean Diet. The Plant-Based Mediterranean Cookbook transforms these humble ingredients into culinary masterpieces. From hearty bean stews to chickpea-based dips, the cookbook showcases the versatility of legumes, providing a satisfying and nutritious alternative to animal proteins.

Healthy fats, particularly olive oil, play a crucial role in the Mediterranean Diet. The Plant-Based Mediterranean Cookbook elevates dishes by incorporating olive oil in various forms, from dressings to sautés. Rich in monounsaturated fats and antioxidants, olive oil not only enhances the flavor of meals but also supports heart health, a key aspect of achieving optimum well-being.

While the Mediterranean Diet encourages the consumption of fish and seafood, the Plant-Based Mediterranean Cookbook caters to those opting for a fully plant-based approach. The cookbook offers inventive recipes using plant-based alternatives such as tofu, tempeh, and plant-based seafood substitutes. These recipes not only align with the diet's principles but also cater to a diverse range of dietary preferences.

Conversely, the Mediterranean Diet advises moderation in red meat consumption. The Plant-Based Mediterranean Cookbook aligns with this guideline, providing recipes that focus on plant-based proteins while minimizing reliance on animal products. This approach not only supports overall health but also aligns with sustainable and ethical considerations associated with plant-based eating.

CHAPTER 2: BENEFITS OF FOLLOWING MEDITERRANEAN DIET

Following a Plant-Based Mediterranean diet offers a myriad of health benefits, combining the best elements of plant-based eating and the traditional Mediterranean diet. *Here are some core benefits:*

1. Heart Health:
Monounsaturated Fats: Olive oil, a staple in the Mediterranean diet, is rich in monounsaturated fats, which have been associated with a reduced risk of cardiovascular diseases. These fats contribute to healthier cholesterol levels and overall heart health.

2. Rich in Antioxidants:
Colorful Fruits and Vegetables: The diet emphasizes a variety of colorful fruits and vegetables, providing a broad spectrum of antioxidants. These compounds help combat

oxidative stress, reduce inflammation, and support overall cellular health.

3. Weight Management:

High Fiber Content: Plant-based foods such as whole grains, legumes, and vegetables are rich in dietary fiber. High-fiber diets are known to promote satiety, aiding in weight management by reducing overeating and promoting a feeling of fullness.

4. Improved Digestive Health:

Fiber-Rich Foods: The abundance of fiber in plant-based foods supports a healthy digestive system. Fiber contributes to regular bowel movements, prevents constipation, and supports a diverse and flourishing gut microbiome.

5. Cancer Prevention:

Antioxidant-Rich Foods: The high intake of antioxidant-rich foods, particularly fruits and vegetables, is associated with a lower risk of certain cancers. The diverse array of phytochemicals in these foods may have protective effects against cancer development.

6. Reduced Inflammation:
Omega-3 Fatty Acids: The inclusion of plant-based sources of omega-3 fatty acids, such as flaxseeds, chia seeds, and walnuts, can help reduce inflammation in the body. Chronic inflammation is linked to various diseases, including heart disease and autoimmune conditions.

7. Diabetes Management:
Whole Grains and Legumes: The complex carbohydrates found in whole grains and legumes have a lower glycemic index, helping to regulate blood sugar levels. This can be beneficial for individuals with diabetes or those at risk of developing the condition.

8. Brain Health:
Healthy Fats: The inclusion of healthy fats, especially omega-3 fatty acids from plant sources, supports cognitive function and

may contribute to a reduced risk of neurodegenerative diseases.

9. Longevity:

Mediterranean Lifestyle: Beyond the diet itself, the Mediterranean lifestyle, which includes regular physical activity, social engagement, and an appreciation for leisure, has been associated with increased longevity. A holistic approach to health is a key aspect of the Plant-Based Mediterranean diet.

10. Sustainable and Environmentally Friendly:

Reduced Environmental Impact: Plant-based diets generally have a lower environmental footprint compared to diets rich in animal products. By emphasizing plant-based foods, the diet aligns with sustainable and eco-friendly practices.

HOW TO FOLLOW MEDITERRANEAN DIET

1. Emphasize Plant-Based Foods:
Fruits and Vegetables: Aim to fill your plate with a colorful array of fruits and vegetables. These provide essential vitamins, minerals, fiber, and antioxidants. Include a variety of leafy greens, berries, tomatoes, cucumbers, and other seasonal produce.

Whole Grains: Opt for whole grains like quinoa, brown rice, bulgur, and whole wheat. These grains are rich in fiber, providing sustained energy and supporting digestive health.

Legumes: Include beans, lentils, chickpeas, and other legumes as primary sources of protein. They are not only nutritious but also contribute to satiety and weight management.

Nuts and Seeds: Incorporate a variety of nuts and seeds, such as almonds, walnuts, chia seeds, and flaxseeds, for healthy fats, protein, and omega-3 fatty acids.

2. Healthy Fats:

Olive Oil: Use extra virgin olive oil as the primary source of fat in cooking and as a salad dressing. Its monounsaturated fats contribute to heart health.

Avocado: Include avocados for additional healthy fats. They are versatile and can be added to salads, spreads, or enjoyed on their own.

3. Lean Proteins:

Plant-Based Proteins: Focus on plant-based protein sources such as tofu, tempeh, and legumes. These provide adequate protein while reducing reliance on animal products.

Fatty Fish (Optional): If you choose to include animal products, consider incorporating fatty fish like salmon or mackerel occasionally for omega-3 fatty acids.

4. Herbs and Spices:

Fresh Herbs: Use a variety of fresh herbs such as basil, oregano, rosemary, and thyme to add flavor to dishes without excessive salt. This enhances the taste while providing additional health benefits.

Spices: Experiment with spices like cumin, coriander, and turmeric to infuse dishes with depth and complexity.

5. Moderate Dairy Intake:

Greek Yogurt and Cheese (Optional): If you include dairy, opt for moderate amounts of Greek yogurt and high-quality cheeses. These can be incorporated into meals or enjoyed as snacks.

6. Limit Processed Foods:

Minimize Processed Foods: Reduce the intake of processed and refined foods.

Choose whole, unprocessed options to maximize nutrient intake and support overall health.

7. Enjoy Regular Physical Activity:

Stay Active: Engage in regular physical activity. The Mediterranean lifestyle places importance on staying active, whether through walking, biking, or participating in recreational activities.

8. Hydrate with Water:

Water as the Primary Beverage: Drink plenty of water throughout the day. Water is the primary beverage in the Mediterranean Diet, and staying well-hydrated is essential for overall health.

9. Socialize and Savor Meals:

Social Meals: Enjoy meals with friends and family. The Mediterranean lifestyle emphasizes the social aspect of meals, creating a positive and enjoyable dining experience.

10. Mindful Eating:

Savor Each Bite: Practice mindful eating by savoring each bite, paying attention to flavors, and listening to your body's hunger and fullness cues.

CHAPTER 3: LIST OF INGREDIENTS

Adopting a Plant-Based Mediterranean diet involves incorporating a variety of wholesome and nutrient-rich ingredients into your meals. Here's a list of 20 healthy shopping ingredients that align with the principles of a Plant-Based Mediterranean diet, perfect for exploring the recipes in a Plant-Based Mediterranean Cookbook:

Fruits and Vegetables

1. Tomatoes: Rich in antioxidants and vitamin C, tomatoes are a staple in Mediterranean cuisine. Use them in salads, sauces, and roasted dishes.

2. Leafy Greens (Spinach, Kale, Arugula): Packed with vitamins, minerals, and fiber, leafy greens add a nutritional boost to salads, wraps, and sautés.

3. Bell Peppers: Colorful bell peppers provide a sweet and crunchy element to various dishes. They are rich in vitamin C and antioxidants.

4. Zucchini and Eggplant: Versatile and low in calories, zucchini and eggplant can be grilled, roasted, or used in casseroles and stews.

5. Berries (Blueberries, Strawberries): These antioxidant-rich fruits add sweetness to breakfasts, desserts, or as a topping for yogurt.

Whole Grains

6. Quinoa: A complete protein source, quinoa is a nutritious grain that can be used as a base for salads, bowls, or side dishes.

7. Bulgur: A quick-cooking whole grain, bulgur is perfect for salads and pilafs, adding fiber and a nutty flavor.

8. Farro: A hearty grain with a chewy texture, farro is excellent in soups, salads, or as a side dish.

Legumes
9. Chickpeas: Versatile and high in protein, chickpeas can be used in salads, stews, and as a base for hummus.

10. Lentils: Packed with fiber and protein, lentils are ideal for soups, stews, and plant-based meat alternatives.

Nuts and Seeds
11. Almonds and Walnuts: These nuts provide healthy fats and can be used in salads, snacks, or as a crunchy topping for dishes.

12. Chia Seeds and Flaxseeds: Rich in omega-3 fatty acids and fiber, these seeds can be added to smoothies, and yogurt, or used in baking.

Healthy Fats

13. Extra Virgin Olive Oil: A cornerstone of the Mediterranean diet, olive oil for cooking, salad dressings, and drizzling over dishes.

14. Avocado: Creamy and nutrient-dense, avocados can be sliced for salads, mashed for spreads, or enjoyed on their own.

Herbs and Spices

15. Basil, Oregano, Rosemary, Thyme: Fresh herbs and aromatic spices add depth and flavor to Mediterranean dishes.

16. Cumin and Coriander: These spices enhance the savory profile of dishes and are commonly used in Mediterranean cooking.

Plant-Based Proteins

17. Tofu and Tempeh: Versatile plant-based proteins that absorb flavors well, suitable for grilling, sautéing, or adding to stir-fries.

18. Plant-Based Seafood Alternatives: For those opting for a fully plant-based

approach, explore options like plant-based shrimp, fish fillets, or crab substitutes.

Dairy Alternatives

19. Almond or Cashew Yogurt: A dairy-free alternative for adding creaminess to dishes or enjoying as a snack.

20. Nutritional Yeast: Adds a cheesy flavor to plant-based dishes and is a source of B vitamins.

CHAPTER 4: HEALTHY RECIPES

Recipe 1: Mediterranean Stuffed Avocado

Ingredients:
- Ripe avocados (2, halved and pitted)
- Cherry tomatoes (1/2 cup, diced)
- Cucumber (1/2 cup, diced)
- Red onion (2 tbsp, finely chopped)
- Kalamata olives (2 tbsp, sliced)
- Fresh parsley (2 tbsp, chopped)
- Olive oil (1 tbsp)
- Lemon juice (1 tbsp)
- Salt and pepper to taste

Instructions:
1. In a bowl, mix diced tomatoes, cucumber, red onion, Kalamata olives, and fresh parsley.

2. Drizzle olive oil and lemon juice over the mixture. Add salt and pepper to taste.
3. Spoon the mixture into the halved avocados.
4. Serve chilled for a refreshing and nutritious Mediterranean breakfast.

Recipe 2: Mediterranean Chia Seed Pudding

Ingredients:
- Chia seeds (1/4 cup)
- Almond milk (1 cup)
- Mixed berries (1/2 cup, such as raspberries and blueberries)
- Pistachios (2 tbsp, chopped)
- Honey (1 tbsp, optional)

Instructions:
1. In a jar, combine chia seeds and almond milk. Stir well and refrigerate overnight.

2. In the morning, layer the chia pudding with mixed berries and chopped pistachios.
3. Drizzle with honey if desired.
4. Enjoy a protein-rich and antioxidant-packed Mediterranean chia seed pudding.

Recipe 3: Mediterranean Breakfast Bruschetta

Ingredients:
- Whole-grain baguette (4 slices, toasted)
- Hummus (1/2 cup)
- Cherry tomatoes (1 cup, diced)
- Red onion (1/4 cup, finely chopped)
- Fresh basil leaves (2 tbsp, chopped)
- Balsamic glaze (1 tbsp)
- Olive oil (1 tbsp)
- Salt and pepper to taste

Instructions:
1. Spread hummus on each toasted baguette slice.
2. In a bowl, mix diced cherry tomatoes, red onion, and fresh basil.
3. Spoon the tomato mixture over the hummus-covered baguette slices.
4. Drizzle with balsamic glaze and olive oil.
5. Season with salt and pepper to taste.
6. Serve as an appetizing and satisfying Mediterranean breakfast.

Recipe 4: Mediterranean Breakfast Burrito

Ingredients:
- Whole-grain tortilla
- Tofu (1/2 cup, crumbled)
- Spinach (1 cup)
- Cherry tomatoes (1/2 cup, sliced)
- Red bell pepper (1/4 cup, diced)
- Kalamata olives (2 tbsp, sliced)
- Fresh dill (1 tbsp, chopped)

- Olive oil (1 tbsp)
- Lemon juice (1 tsp)
- Salt and pepper to taste

Instructions:
1. In a pan, sauté crumbled tofu in olive oil until lightly browned.
2. Add spinach, cherry tomatoes, red bell pepper, and Kalamata olives to the pan. Sauté until the spinach wilts.
3. Drizzle with lemon juice, and season with salt, pepper, and fresh dill.
4. Spoon the mixture onto a whole-grain tortilla, fold, and enjoy a hearty Mediterranean breakfast burrito.

Recipe 5: Greek-Inspired Overnight Oats

Ingredients:
- Rolled oats (1/2 cup)
- Almond milk (1/2 cup)
- Greek yogurt (1/4 cup)

- Mixed berries (1/2 cup, such as strawberries and blueberries)
- Walnuts (2 tbsp, chopped)
- Honey (1 tbsp, optional)

Instructions:
1. In a jar, combine rolled oats, almond milk, and Greek yogurt. Stir well and refrigerate overnight.
2. In the morning, top the oats with mixed berries and chopped walnuts.
3. Drizzle with honey if desired.
4. Enjoy a protein-packed and satisfying Greek-inspired breakfast.

LUNCH

Recipe 1: Mediterranean Quinoa Salad

Ingredients:

- Quinoa (1 cup, cooked)
- Cherry tomatoes (1 cup, halved)
- Cucumber (1/2 cup, diced)
- Red bell pepper (1/2 cup, diced)
- Kalamata olives (1/4 cup, sliced)
- Red onion (2 tbsp, finely chopped)
- Fresh parsley (2 tbsp, chopped)
- Extra virgin olive oil (2 tbsp)
- Lemon juice (2 tbsp)
- Dried oregano (1 tsp)
- Salt and pepper to taste

Instructions:

1. In a large bowl, combine cooked quinoa, cherry tomatoes, cucumber, red bell pepper, Kalamata olives, red onion, and fresh parsley.

2. In a small bowl, whisk together olive oil, lemon juice, dried oregano, salt, and pepper.
3. Drizzle the dressing over the salad and toss to combine.
4. Chill in the refrigerator for at least 30 minutes before serving.
5. Serve as a refreshing and nutrient-rich Mediterranean quinoa salad.

Recipe 2: Mediterranean Chickpea and Vegetable Skewers

Ingredients:
- Chickpeas (1 can, drained and rinsed)
- Cherry tomatoes (1 cup)
- Red onion (1, cut into chunks)
- Zucchini (1, sliced)
- Bell peppers (assorted colors, 1 cup, cut into chunks)
- Olive oil (2 tbsp)
- Garlic powder (1 tsp)
- Dried oregano (1 tsp)

- Lemon juice (2 tbsp)
- Salt and pepper to taste

Instructions:

1. Preheat the oven to 400°F (200°C) or prepare a grill.
2. In a bowl, mix chickpeas, cherry tomatoes, red onion, zucchini, and bell peppers.
3. In a small bowl, whisk together olive oil, garlic powder, dried oregano, lemon juice, salt, and pepper.
4. Thread the vegetable and chickpea mixture onto skewers.
5. Brush the skewers with the prepared marinade.
6. Bake in the oven or grill until vegetables are tender and lightly charred.
7. Serve the skewers as a flavorful and protein-packed Mediterranean lunch.

Recipe 3: Mediterranean Stuffed Bell Peppers

Ingredients:

- Bell peppers (4, halved and seeds removed)
- Quinoa (1 cup, cooked)
- Cannellini beans (1 can, drained and rinsed)
- Spinach (1 cup, chopped)
- Cherry tomatoes (1/2 cup, diced)
- Red onion (2 tbsp, finely chopped)
- Kalamata olives (2 tbsp, sliced)
- Fresh basil (2 tbsp, chopped)
- Olive oil (2 tbsp)
- Balsamic vinegar (1 tbsp)
- Salt and pepper to taste

Instructions:

1. Preheat the oven to 375°F (190°C).
2. In a bowl, combine cooked quinoa, cannellini beans, chopped spinach, diced cherry tomatoes, red onion, Kalamata olives, and fresh basil.

3. Drizzle with olive oil and balsamic vinegar. Season with salt and pepper.
4. Spoon the mixture into halved bell peppers.
5. Bake for 25-30 minutes or until peppers are tender.
6. Serve as a satisfying and wholesome Mediterranean stuffed bell pepper dish.

Recipe 4: Greek Chickpea Salad Wraps

Ingredients:
- Whole-grain wraps
- Chickpeas (1 can, drained and mashed)
- Cucumber (1/2 cup, diced)
- Cherry tomatoes (1/2 cup, halved)
- Red onion (2 tbsp, finely chopped)
- Kalamata olives (2 tbsp, sliced)
- Fresh parsley (2 tbsp, chopped)
- Vegan tzatziki sauce (store-bought or homemade)

- Olive oil (1 tbsp)
- Lemon juice (1 tbsp)
- Salt and pepper to taste

Instructions:

1. In a bowl, mix mashed chickpeas, diced cucumber, halved cherry tomatoes, red onion, Kalamata olives, and fresh parsley.
2. In a small bowl, whisk together olive oil, lemon juice, salt, and pepper.
3. Spoon the chickpea mixture onto whole-grain wraps.
4. Drizzle with vegan tzatziki sauce and the prepared dressing.
5. Roll the wraps tightly and slice them in half.
6. Enjoy a flavorful and protein-rich Greek chickpea salad wrap.

Recipe 5: Mediterranean Lentil Soup

Ingredients:

- Green lentils (1 cup, dried)
- Carrots (2, diced)
- Celery (2 stalks, diced)
- Onion (1, finely chopped)
- Garlic (3 cloves, minced)
- Tomato paste (2 tbsp)
- Vegetable broth (4 cups)
- Cumin (1 tsp)
- Smoked paprika (1 tsp)
- Bay leaves (2)
- Fresh lemon juice (2 tbsp)
- Fresh parsley (2 tbsp, chopped)
- Olive oil (2 tbsp)
- Salt and pepper to taste

Instructions:

1. Rinse and drain the green lentils.
2. In a large pot, heat olive oil and sauté onions, garlic, carrots, and celery until softened.
3. Add tomato paste, cumin, and smoked paprika. Stir to coat the vegetables.
4. Pour in vegetable broth and add bay leaves. Bring to a boil.
5. Add green lentils, reduce heat, and simmer until lentils are tender.
6. Stir in fresh lemon juice, chopped parsley, salt, and pepper.
7. Remove bay leaves before serving.
8. Enjoy a hearty and nourishing Mediterranean lentil soup.

SNACKS

Recipe 1: Hummus and Veggie Platter

Ingredients:
- Hummus (1 cup, store-bought or homemade)
- Baby carrots (1 cup)
- Cucumber (1, sliced)
- Cherry tomatoes (1 cup, halved)
- Bell pepper strips (assorted colors, 1 cup)
- Kalamata olives (1/4 cup)
- Whole-grain pita bread (cut into triangles)

Instructions:
1. Arrange hummus in the center of a serving platter.
2. Surround the hummus with baby carrots, cucumber slices, cherry tomatoes, bell pepper strips, and Kalamata olives.

3. Serve with whole-grain pita bread on the side.
4. Dip and enjoy this Mediterranean-inspired veggie platter.

Recipe 2: Mediterranean Stuffed Grape Leaves

Ingredients:
- Grape leaves (1 jar, drained)
- Cooked quinoa (1 cup)
- Chickpeas (1/2 cup, cooked and mashed)
- Sun-dried tomatoes (2 tbsp, chopped)
- Fresh parsley (2 tbsp, chopped)
- Lemon juice (2 tbsp)
- Olive oil (2 tbsp)
- Garlic powder (1 tsp)
- Salt and pepper to taste

Instructions:
1. In a bowl, mix cooked quinoa, mashed chickpeas, sun-dried tomatoes, fresh parsley, lemon juice,

olive oil, garlic powder, salt, and pepper.
2. Place a grape leaf on a flat surface and spoon the quinoa mixture onto the center.
3. Fold the sides of the grape leaf over the filling and roll tightly.
4. Repeat with the remaining grape leaves and filling.
5. Chill in the refrigerator for at least 30 minutes before serving.
6. Enjoy these refreshing and tangy Mediterranean-stuffed grape leaves.

Recipe 3: Greek Salad Skewers

Ingredients:
- Cherry tomatoes (1 cup)
- Cucumber (1/2 cup, diced)
- Vegan feta cheese (1/2 cup, cubed)
- Kalamata olives (1/4 cup)
- Red onion (1/4 cup, sliced)
- Fresh basil leaves (2 tbsp)

- Olive oil (2 tbsp)
- Balsamic glaze (1 tbsp)
- Skewers

Instructions:
1. Thread cherry tomatoes, cucumber, vegan feta cheese, Kalamata olives, and red onion onto skewers.
2. In a small bowl, whisk together olive oil and balsamic glaze.
3. Drizzle the dressing over the skewers.
4. Garnish with fresh basil leaves.
5. Serve these Greek salad skewers as a delightful and easy-to-eat snack.

Recipe 4: Roasted Red Pepper and Walnut Dip

Ingredients:
- Roasted red peppers (1 cup, jarred or homemade)
- Walnuts (1/2 cup, toasted)
- Garlic (2 cloves)
- Olive oil (2 tbsp)

- Lemon juice (2 tbsp)
- Smoked paprika (1 tsp)
- Cumin (1/2 tsp)
- Salt and pepper to taste
- Whole-grain crackers or veggie sticks for dipping

Instructions:
1. In a food processor, combine roasted red peppers, toasted walnuts, garlic, olive oil, lemon juice, smoked paprika, cumin, salt, and pepper.
2. Blend until smooth and creamy.
3. Adjust seasonings to taste.
4. Transfer to a bowl and serve with whole-grain crackers or veggie sticks.
5. Enjoy this flavorful and nutritious roasted red pepper and walnut dip.

Recipe 5: Mediterranean Fruit Salad

Ingredients:
- Watermelon (1 cup, cubed)
- Cantaloupe (1 cup, cubed)
- Grapes (1 cup, halved)
- Mint leaves (2 tbsp, chopped)
- Lemon zest (1 tsp)
- Balsamic glaze (1 tbsp)
- Pistachios (2 tbsp, chopped)

Instructions:
1. In a large bowl, combine watermelon, cantaloupe, and grapes.
2. Sprinkle chopped mint leaves and lemon zest over the fruit.
3. Drizzle with balsamic glaze and toss gently to combine.
4. Garnish with chopped pistachios before serving.
5. Enjoy this refreshing and sweet Mediterranean fruit salad.

DINNER

Recipe 1: Mediterranean Chickpea and Spinach Stew

Ingredients:

- Chickpeas (2 cans, drained and rinsed)
- Spinach (4 cups, chopped)
- Tomatoes (2 cups, diced)
- Red onion (1, finely chopped)
- Garlic (4 cloves, minced)
- Vegetable broth (3 cups)
- Olive oil (2 tbsp)
- Ground cumin (1 tsp)
- Smoked paprika (1 tsp)
- Lemon juice (2 tbsp)
- Fresh parsley (2 tbsp, chopped)
- Salt and pepper to taste

Instructions:

1. In a large pot, sauté red onion and garlic in olive oil until softened.
2. Add diced tomatoes, chickpeas, chopped spinach, vegetable broth, cumin, smoked paprika, salt, and pepper.
3. Bring to a simmer and cook for 20-25 minutes.
4. Stir in lemon juice and fresh parsley before serving.
5. Enjoy this hearty and flavorful Mediterranean chickpea and spinach stew.

Recipe 2: Stuffed Portobello Mushrooms

Ingredients:

- Portobello mushrooms (4, stems removed)
- Quinoa (1 cup, cooked)
- Sun-dried tomatoes (1/2 cup, chopped)

- Baby spinach (2 cups)
- Red onion (1/4 cup, finely chopped)
- Vegan feta cheese (1/4 cup, crumbled)
- Balsamic vinegar (2 tbsp)
- Olive oil (2 tbsp)
- Fresh basil (2 tbsp, chopped)
- Salt and pepper to taste

Instructions:
1. Preheat the oven to 375°F (190°C).
2. In a bowl, mix cooked quinoa, sun-dried tomatoes, baby spinach, red onion, vegan feta, balsamic vinegar, olive oil, salt, and pepper.
3. Spoon the quinoa mixture into the hollowed Portobello mushrooms.
4. Place the mushrooms on a baking sheet and bake for 20-25 minutes.
5. Garnish with chopped fresh basil before serving.
6. Enjoy these stuffed Portobello mushrooms as a satisfying and elegant dinner option.

Recipe 3: Mediterranean Lentil and Vegetable Stir-Fry

Ingredients:

- Green lentils (1 cup, dried)
- Broccoli florets (2 cups)
- Bell peppers (assorted colors, 1 cup, sliced)
- Cherry tomatoes (1/2 cup, halved)
- Red onion (1, sliced)
- Garlic (3 cloves, minced)
- Olive oil (2 tbsp)
- Lemon juice (2 tbsp)
- Fresh oregano (1 tbsp, chopped)
- Salt and pepper to taste

Instructions:

1. Cook green lentils according to package instructions.
2. In a large pan, sauté garlic in olive oil until fragrant.
3. Add broccoli, bell peppers, cherry tomatoes, and red onion. Stir-fry until vegetables are tender-crisp.

4. Stir in cooked lentils, lemon juice, fresh oregano, salt, and pepper.
5. Cook for an additional 2-3 minutes.
6. Serve this Mediterranean lentil and vegetable stir-fry warm.

Recipe 4: Greek-Inspired Couscous Salad

Ingredients:
- Whole wheat couscous (1 cup, cooked)
- Chickpeas (1 can, drained and rinsed)
- Cucumber (1, diced)
- Cherry tomatoes (1 cup, halved)
- Kalamata olives (1/2 cup, sliced)
- Red onion (1/4 cup, finely chopped)
- Vegan feta cheese (1/4 cup, crumbled)
- Olive oil (2 tbsp)
- Lemon juice (2 tbsp)
- Fresh dill (2 tbsp, chopped)
- Salt and pepper to taste

Instructions:

1. In a large bowl, combine cooked couscous, chickpeas, diced cucumber, cherry tomatoes, Kalamata olives, red onion, and vegan feta.
2. In a small bowl, whisk together olive oil, lemon juice, fresh dill, salt, and pepper.
3. Pour the dressing over the couscous mixture and toss to combine.
4. Chill in the refrigerator for at least 30 minutes before serving.
5. Enjoy this refreshing and protein-packed Greek-inspired couscous salad.

Recipe 5: Eggplant and Tomato Bake

Ingredients:

- Eggplant (2, sliced into rounds)
- Tomatoes (3 cups, sliced)
- Red onion (1, sliced)
- Garlic (4 cloves, minced)

- Fresh basil leaves (1/2 cup)
- Olive oil (3 tbsp)
- Balsamic vinegar (2 tbsp)
- Vegan mozzarella cheese (1/2 cup, shredded)
- Salt and pepper to taste

Instructions:
1. Preheat the oven to 375°F (190°C).
2. In a baking dish, layer eggplant slices, tomato slices, and red onion.
3. In a small bowl, mix minced garlic, fresh basil, olive oil, balsamic vinegar, salt, and pepper.
4. Drizzle the garlic and basil mixture over the vegetables.
5. Sprinkle vegan mozzarella cheese on top.
6. Bake for 30-35 minutes or until the vegetables are tender and the cheese is melted and bubbly.
7. Serve this savory and comforting eggplant and tomato bake.

DESSERT

Recipe 1: Mediterranean Fruit Salad with Mint

Ingredients:
- Mixed fruits (2 cups, such as watermelon, cantaloupe, grapes, and berries)
- Fresh mint leaves (2 tbsp, chopped)
- Honey or agave syrup (1-2 tbsp, optional)

Instructions:
1. Combine mixed fruits in a bowl.
2. Sprinkle chopped mint leaves over the fruits.
3. Drizzle with honey or agave syrup if desired.
4. Gently toss the fruits and mint together.
5. Chill in the refrigerator for at least 30 minutes before serving.
6. Enjoy this refreshing and naturally sweet Mediterranean fruit salad.

Recipe 2: Greek Yogurt Parfait with Pistachios and Honey

Ingredients:

- Greek yogurt (1 cup)
- Mixed berries (1/2 cup, such as strawberries and blueberries)
- Pistachios (2 tbsp, chopped)
- Honey (1 tbsp)

Instructions:

1. In a glass or bowl, layer Greek yogurt at the bottom.
2. Add a layer of mixed berries on top of the yogurt.
3. Sprinkle chopped pistachios over the berries.
4. Drizzle with honey.
5. Repeat the layers until the glass or bowl is filled.
6. Serve this creamy and nutritious Greek yogurt parfait.

Recipe 3: Almond and Orange Blossom Cookies

Ingredients:

- Almond flour (1 cup)
- Coconut oil (1/4 cup, melted)
- Maple syrup (1/4 cup)
- Orange blossom water (1 tsp)
- Almond extract (1/2 tsp)
- Orange zest (1 tbsp)
- Sliced almonds (2 tbsp, for topping)

Instructions:

1. Preheat the oven to 350°F (175°C) and line a baking sheet with parchment paper.
2. In a bowl, mix almond flour, melted coconut oil, maple syrup, orange blossom water, almond extract, and orange zest until a dough forms.
3. Scoop tablespoon-sized portions of dough and roll them into balls.
4. Place the balls on the prepared baking sheet, flattening each with a fork.

5. Top each cookie with a few sliced almonds.
6. Bake for 10-12 minutes or until the edges are golden brown.
7. Allow the cookies to cool before serving.

Recipe 4: Date and Walnut Energy Bites

Ingredients:
- Dates (1 cup, pitted)
- Walnuts (1/2 cup)
- Almond butter (2 tbsp)
- Rolled oats (1/4 cup)
- Cinnamon (1 tsp)
- Shredded coconut (1/4 cup, for coating)

Instructions:
1. In a food processor, blend dates, walnuts, almond butter, rolled oats, and cinnamon until a sticky dough forms.

2. Scoop out tablespoon-sized portions of the dough and roll them into balls.
3. Roll each ball in shredded coconut to coat.
4. Place the energy bites on a tray and refrigerate for at least 30 minutes.
5. Serve these wholesome date and walnut energy bites.

Recipe 5: Vegan Lemon Sorbet

Ingredients:
- Lemon juice (1 cup, freshly squeezed)
- Water (1 cup)
- Maple syrup or agave syrup (1/2 cup)
- Lemon zest (1 tbsp)

Instructions:
1. In a bowl, mix freshly squeezed lemon juice, water, maple syrup or agave syrup, and lemon zest.

2. Pour the mixture into an ice cream maker and churn according to the manufacturer's instructions.
3. Once churned, transfer the sorbet to a container and freeze for at least 4 hours or until firm.
4. Scoop and serve this refreshing vegan lemon sorbet.

CHAPTER 5: MEAL PLANNING

Meal planning for a Plant-Based Mediterranean diet involves strategizing and organizing your daily and weekly meals to align with the principles of this dietary pattern. The Plant-Based Mediterranean diet emphasizes whole, plant-based foods and incorporates elements inspired by the traditional eating patterns of countries bordering the Mediterranean Sea. The diet emphasizes fruits, vegetables, whole grains, legumes, nuts, seeds, and olive oil while minimizing processed foods and red meat.

Benefits of Meal Planning

(for a Plant-Based Mediterranean Diet Cookbook)

1. Nutrient-Rich Meals:
Plant-based foods are rich in essential nutrients such as vitamins, minerals, fiber, and antioxidants.
Incorporating a variety of colorful fruits and vegetables ensures a diverse range of nutrients that contribute to overall health.

2. Heart Health:
The Mediterranean diet is renowned for its heart-healthy benefits, attributed to the consumption of olive oil, nuts, and seeds, which are sources of monounsaturated and polyunsaturated fats.
These healthy fats help reduce the risk of cardiovascular diseases.

3. Weight Management:
A plant-based diet is naturally lower in calories and saturated fats, making it

suitable for those looking to manage or lose weight.
The emphasis on whole, unprocessed foods helps control calorie intake while providing essential nutrients.

4. Digestive Health:
The high fiber content in plant-based foods supports digestive health by promoting regular bowel movements and a healthy gut microbiome.
Legumes, whole grains, fruits, and vegetables are excellent sources of dietary fiber.

5. Inflammation Reduction:
The anti-inflammatory properties of many plant-based foods can help reduce inflammation in the body.
Consuming omega-3 fatty acids from sources like walnuts and flaxseeds further contributes to inflammation reduction.

6. Disease Prevention:

The Mediterranean diet has been associated with a lower risk of chronic diseases such as type 2 diabetes, certain cancers, and neurodegenerative conditions.
The abundance of antioxidants in plant-based foods plays a role in disease prevention.

7. Sustainability:

A plant-based diet aligns with sustainability goals by reducing the environmental impact associated with animal agriculture.
Choosing local, seasonal produce further supports sustainable eating practices.

Tips for Effective Meal Planning

1. Variety is Key:
Include a variety of fruits, vegetables, whole grains, legumes, nuts, and seeds to ensure a diverse nutrient profile and prevent monotony.

2. Batch Cooking:
Prepare larger quantities of staple items like grains, beans, and roasted vegetables, making it easier to assemble meals throughout the week.

3. Weekly Planning:
Plan your meals for the week ahead, taking into consideration your schedule, activities, and available ingredients.

4. Prep Ingredients in Advance:
Wash, chop, and prep vegetables and fruits in advance to streamline the cooking process during busy days.

5. Mindful Eating:
Practice mindful eating by savoring each bite, paying attention to hunger and fullness cues, and enjoying meals without distractions.

6. Experiment with Flavors:
Incorporate Mediterranean herbs and spices, such as basil, oregano, thyme, and rosemary, to enhance the flavors of your dishes.

7. Balance Macronutrients:
Ensure a balance of carbohydrates, proteins, and healthy fats in your meals for sustained energy and satiety.

8. Hydration:
Hydrate with water and incorporate herbal teas. Limit sugary beverages and alcohol.

9. Seasonal and Local Choices:
Choose seasonal and locally sourced produce when possible for optimal freshness and environmental sustainability.

By adopting a Plant-Based Mediterranean diet and implementing effective meal planning, individuals can enjoy a wide range of health benefits while maintaining a balanced and satisfying approach to eating. The combination of nutrient-rich foods and mindful meal planning supports overall well-being and longevity.

14-DAY MEAL PLAN

Day 1:
Breakfast: Mediterranean Stuffed Avocado
Snack: Hummus and Veggie Platter
Lunch: Mediterranean Quinoa Salad
Snack: Greek Salad Skewers
Dinner: Mediterranean Chickpea and Spinach Stew

Day 2:
Breakfast: Quinoa Breakfast Bowl
Snack: Mediterranean Stuffed Grape Leaves
Lunch: Stuffed Portobello Mushrooms
Snack: Roasted Red Pepper and Walnut Dip with Veggie Sticks
Dinner: Greek-inspired couscous Salad

Day 3:
Breakfast: Mediterranean Chickpea Omelette
Snack: Greek Salad Skewers
Lunch: Mediterranean Lentil and Vegetable Stir-Fry
Snack: Mediterranean Fruit Salad with Mint

Dinner: Eggplant and Tomato Bake

Day 4:
Breakfast: Greek-Inspired Overnight Oats
Snack: Hummus and Veggie Platter
Lunch: Greek Chickpea Salad Wraps
Snack: Almond and Orange Blossom Cookies
Dinner: Mediterranean Quinoa Salad

Day 5:
Breakfast: Mediterranean Breakfast Wrap
Snack: Mediterranean Stuffed Grape Leaves
Lunch: Greek-inspired couscous Salad
Snack: Date and Walnut Energy Bites
Dinner: Stuffed Portobello Mushrooms

Day 6:
Breakfast: Quinoa Breakfast Bowl
Snack: Greek Salad Skewers
Lunch: Mediterranean Stuffed Bell Peppers
Snack: Roasted Red Pepper and Walnut Dip with Veggie Sticks
Dinner: Greek-inspired couscous Salad

Day 7:
Breakfast: Mediterranean Avocado Toast
Snack: Hummus and Veggie Platter
Lunch: Mediterranean Lentil Soup
Snack: Almond and Orange Blossom Cookies
Dinner: Eggplant and Tomato Bake

Day 8:
Breakfast: Greek-Inspired Overnight Oats
Snack: Greek Salad Skewers
Lunch: Greek Chickpea Salad Wraps
Snack: Mediterranean Fruit Salad with Mint
Dinner: Mediterranean Quinoa Salad

Day 9:
Breakfast: Mediterranean Stuffed Avocado
Snack: Date and Walnut Energy Bites
Lunch: Stuffed Portobello Mushrooms
Snack: Roasted Red Pepper and Walnut Dip with Veggie Sticks
Dinner: Mediterranean Chickpea and Spinach Stew

Day 10:
Breakfast: Quinoa Breakfast Bowl
Snack: Hummus and Veggie Platter
Lunch: Mediterranean Lentil and Vegetable Stir-Fry
Snack: Almond and Orange Blossom Cookies
Dinner: Greek-inspired couscous Salad

Day 11:
Breakfast: Greek-Inspired Overnight Oats
Snack: Greek Salad Skewers
Lunch: Mediterranean Stuffed Bell Peppers
Snack: Mediterranean Fruit Salad with Mint
Dinner: Eggplant and Tomato Bake

Day 12:
Breakfast: Mediterranean Avocado Toast
Snack: Date and Walnut Energy Bites
Lunch: Greek Chickpea Salad Wraps
Snack: Roasted Red Pepper and Walnut Dip with Veggie Sticks
Dinner: Mediterranean Quinoa Salad

Day 13:
Breakfast: Quinoa Breakfast Bowl
Snack: Greek Salad Skewers
Lunch: Stuffed Portobello Mushrooms
Snack: Almond and Orange Blossom Cookies
Dinner: Greek-inspired couscous Salad

Day 14:
Breakfast: Mediterranean Chickpea Omelette
Snack: Hummus and Veggie Platter
Lunch: Mediterranean Lentil Soup
Snack: Mediterranean Fruit Salad with Mint
Dinner: Eggplant and Tomato Bake

CONCLUSION

In conclusion, this Plant-Based Mediterranean Diet Cookbook offers a flavorful journey toward optimal health and well-being. Rooted in the bountiful traditions of the Mediterranean, the cookbook emphasizes the vibrant colors, rich flavors, and nutritional benefits of plant-based eating. With a diverse array of recipes spanning breakfast, lunch, dinner, snacks, and desserts, this cookbook provides a holistic approach to nourishing your body.

By embracing the Mediterranean lifestyle, you not only embark on a culinary adventure but also cultivate habits associated with longevity and vitality. The fusion of fresh fruits, vegetables, whole grains, and heart-healthy fats not only supports weight management but also promotes cardiovascular health, digestive well-being, and inflammation reduction.

As you explore these delectable recipes, consider this journey as an investment in your long-term health. The harmony of plant-based ingredients not only tantalizes your taste buds but also nurtures your body from the inside out. Remember, the Mediterranean lifestyle is not just a diet – it's a celebration of wholesome, life-enriching choices.

So, let these recipes be your guide to a more vibrant, energetic you. Let each meal be a step towards a healthier, happier life. As you embark on this culinary adventure, may the flavors of the Mediterranean inspire you to adopt and adapt, making every dish a celebration of well-being. Your journey to a healthier lifestyle starts with a single, delicious bite. Bon appétit and cheers to your well-deserved health and vitality!

BONUS: WEEKLY MEAL PLANNER/ JOURNAL

MEAL PLANNER

Weekly

WEEK _____   MONTH _____

MONDAY

SATURDAY

TUESDAY

SUNDAY

WEDNESDAY

SHOPPING LIST

- ○ _____
- ○ _____
- ○ _____
- ○ _____

THURSDAY

- ○ _____
- ○ _____
- ○ _____
- ○ _____
- ○ _____

FRIDAY

- ○ _____
- ○ _____
- ○ _____
- ○ _____

MEAL PLANNER

Weekly

WEEK _____   MONTH _____

MONDAY

SATURDAY

TUESDAY

SUNDAY

WEDNESDAY

SHOPPING LIST

○ _____
○ _____
○ _____
○ _____
○ _____
○ _____

THURSDAY

○ _____
○ _____
○ _____
○ _____

FRIDAY

○ _____
○ _____
○ _____
○ _____

MEAL PLANNER

Weekly

WEEK _____   MONTH _____

MONDAY

SATURDAY

TUESDAY

SUNDAY

WEDNESDAY

SHOPPING LIST

- ○ _____
- ○ _____
- ○ _____
- ○ _____
- ○ _____

THURSDAY

- ○ _____
- ○ _____
- ○ _____
- ○ _____

FRIDAY

- ○ _____
- ○ _____
- ○ _____
- ○ _____

85

MEAL PLANNER

Weekly

WEEK _____   MONTH _____

MONDAY

SATURDAY

TUESDAY

SUNDAY

WEDNESDAY

SHOPPING LIST
- ○ _____
- ○ _____
- ○ _____
- ○ _____
- ○ _____
- ○ _____
- ○ _____
- ○ _____
- ○ _____
- ○ _____
- ○ _____
- ○ _____
- ○ _____

THURSDAY

FRIDAY

MEAL PLANNER

Weekly

WEEK _____   MONTH _____

MONDAY

TUESDAY

WEDNESDAY

THURSDAY

FRIDAY

SATURDAY

SUNDAY

SHOPPING LIST

- ○ _____
- ○ _____
- ○ _____
- ○ _____
- ○ _____
- ○ _____
- ○ _____
- ○ _____
- ○ _____
- ○ _____
- ○ _____
- ○ _____

MEAL PLANNER

Weekly

WEEK _____   MONTH _____

MONDAY

SATURDAY

TUESDAY

SUNDAY

WEDNESDAY

SHOPPING LIST

- ○ _____
- ○ _____
- ○ _____
- ○ _____

THURSDAY

- ○ _____
- ○ _____
- ○ _____
- ○ _____

FRIDAY

- ○ _____
- ○ _____
- ○ _____
- ○ _____

MEAL PLANNER

Weekly

WEEK _____   MONTH _____

MONDAY	SATURDAY

TUESDAY	SUNDAY

WEDNESDAY

THURSDAY

FRIDAY

SHOPPING LIST

○ _____
○ _____
○ _____
○ _____
○ _____
○ _____
○ _____
○ _____
○ _____
○ _____
○ _____
○ _____
○ _____

MEAL
PLANNER

Weekly

WEEK _____ MONTH _____

MONDAY

SATURDAY

TUESDAY

SUNDAY

WEDNESDAY

SHOPPING LIST
- ○ _____
- ○ _____
- ○ _____
- ○ _____

THURSDAY
- ○ _____
- ○ _____
- ○ _____
- ○ _____

FRIDAY
- ○ _____
- ○ _____
- ○ _____
- ○ _____

MEAL PLANNER

Weekly

WEEK _____   MONTH _____

MONDAY

TUESDAY

WEDNESDAY

THURSDAY

FRIDAY

SATURDAY

SUNDAY

SHOPPING LIST

- ○ _____
- ○ _____
- ○ _____
- ○ _____
- ○ _____
- ○ _____
- ○ _____
- ○ _____
- ○ _____
- ○ _____
- ○ _____
- ○ _____
- ○ _____

MEAL PLANNER

Weekly

WEEK _____   MONTH _____

MONDAY

SATURDAY

TUESDAY

SUNDAY

WEDNESDAY

SHOPPING LIST
- ○ _____
- ○ _____
- ○ _____
- ○ _____

THURSDAY
- ○ _____
- ○ _____
- ○ _____
- ○ _____

FRIDAY
- ○ _____
- ○ _____
- ○ _____
- ○ _____

Printed in the USA
CPSIA information can be obtained
at www.ICGtesting.com
LVHW010044280524
781562LV00006B/368